Text and Illustrations copyright © 2021 Erica Mitra

All rights reserved.
No part of this publication may be reproduced, distributed, or transmitted in any form or by any means, including photocopying, recording, or other electronic or mechanical methods, without the prior written permission of the publisher, except in the case of brief quotations embodied in reviews and certain other noncommercial uses permitted by copyright law.

The resources in this book are provided for informational purposes only and should not be used to replace the specialized training and professional judgment of a health care or mental health care professional.
Neither the author nor the publisher can be held responsible for the use of the information provided within this book. Please always consult a trained professional before making any decision regarding treatment of yourself or others.

The moral right of the author and illustrator has been asserted.

Cover design and illustrations by Alexis Glugla
Hardback ISBN-13: 978-1-7365690-0-9
Paperback ISBN-13: 978-1-7365690-2-3
eBook ISBN-13: 978-1-7365690-1-6

Library of Congress Control Number: 2021902945

Mitra, Erica
A Kiss in My Heart: Hope for Co-Parenting/ Erica Mitra
Ryan has a happy family, but when his routines and environment begin changing, so do his feelings. He starts to wonder where happy went. A Kiss in My Heart is for families of young children who are experiencing divorce or separation. When love is given, happiness can be found again.

ISBN-(hc) 13: 978-1-7365690-0-9

DEDICATION

For my son Rihaan, I love you more than words can express.
For the kiddos, may you learn to find the good in all the places you go.

~ EM

To my cousin Rihaan, may you always seek love in everything that you do
and always look up to those who surround you. I love you!

~ AG

Hi, I am Ryan! Here is my family.
We all love each other.

We drive in the car.

Momma and Dadda don't talk. It is quiet.

I eat dinner in the kitchen.
Momma seems angry. Dadda seems angry.

I get ready for bed again... Where is happy?

Momma picks me up from Grandma and Grandpa's...

Momma says, "We're going to have two houses, Momma's house and Dadda's house." I am confused.

I get tucked into bed for the night. I hear Dadda leave. I chase Dadda and bump my head. OUCH!

Momma and I eat breakfast.

Where is Dadda? I am sad.

Momma says, "You'll have two sleeps at Dadda's house." I'm excited.

I grab my blue bear.

Momma and I drive to Dadda's new house.
I am quiet.

Momma says, "I'll blow you a kiss. Catch it! Put it in your heart!" I put it in my heart. I feel loved.

I play with Momma. I miss Dadda, but I remember that I have his kiss in my heart. I feel content.

It's not bad having two houses.
At Dadda's house we go on adventures.

Here I am at school. Momma's kiss in my heart, and Dadda's kiss in my heart!

**Their love goes with me everywhere.
I feel safe and happy!**

QUESTIONS FOR REFLECTION

It is important to recognize our emotions as they come and go. Below are some discussion questions for you and your child or student.

What different emotions does Ryan experience?

Have you ever had the same emotions? When and why?

What does Ryan's Mom and Dad do that is the same?

What does Ryan's Mom and Dad do that is different?

A NOTE OF THANKS

To Parents- Thank you for sharing this story with your little one(s). My hope is that they learn how to identify their emotions just as Ryan did. Once we can identify an emotion, and speak about it we can let it pass.

To Teachers- Thank you for seeing the value in discussing at-home matters at school and offering a safe place for children to talk about different living situations. It is important for them to realize that other classmates and friends may be experiencing changes in their living environments.

AUTHOR

Erica Mitra loves drawing, playing the piano, eating healthy foods and dancing around her house with her son. Erica is a Fitness and Wellness Coordinator for Detroit Medical Center, a Certified Brain Health Coach, Exercise Specialist and Group Fitness Instructor. She lives in Ferndale, Michigan.

ILLUSTRATOR

Alexis Glugla is a woman who wants to pursue a career in the graphic design industry. Alexis enjoys drawings, exploring the outdoors, playing video games, and spending time with family and friends. Alexis is currently a student at Wayne State University, and is a part-time waitress. She plans on working wherever her future career takes her. She lives in Macomb, Michigan.

Made in the USA
Monee, IL
28 January 2023

26565389R00021